MY BIBLE

for *Preschoolers*

written by
Ellen W. Caughey

illustrated by
Kathy Arbuckle

A Barbour Book

 Member of the
Evangelical Christian
Publishers Association

Published by Barbour and Company, Inc.
            P.O. Box 719
            Uhrichsville, Ohio 44683

Printed in Hong Kong.

To our
children,
Andy, Hannah,
and Nathan

Ellen and Kathy

Contents

Old Testament Stories

New Testament Stories

Introduction

Did you know Jesus proclaimed that the very kingdom of God belongs to little children? Jesus went on to say that anyone who does not receive God's Word with the innocence of a child will never spend eternity with Him.

My Bible for Preschoolers is a place to begin a child's spiritual journey. Thumbnail sketches of forty Bible stories are offered, with each accompanied by an imaginative illustration. Each story concludes with a simple statement that reinforces a biblical principle.

Every story marks a tiny step toward a life lived for Jesus Christ. And every moment spent sharing God's Word with a young friend is surely time blessed by our Heavenly Father.

Old Testament Stories

from the Old Testament

God Makes Everything

A long time ago God decided to make a beautiful world. Your world.

A long time ago there was only God. So only God could make everything.

In six days God made the earth and oceans, plants and trees, the sun, moon, and stars, animals, and people. On the seventh day, the day we call Sunday, God rested.

God named the first man Adam and first woman Eve. Together with all the animals, even lions and tigers, Adam and Eve lived happily in the Garden of Eden.

Remember:
God made you, too.

from the Old Testament

One Good Man

Many years after Adam and Eve lived the world had become a scary place. Only one man listened to God. Only one man loved God. His name was Noah.

So God decided to send a big rain to wash away the earth. Only Noah and his family, and two of every animal on earth, would be saved. God would save them all in a big boat called an **ark.** Even though his neighbors laughed at him Noah kept on building the ark until it was exactly the way God wanted.

After many days of rain everyone on the ark was safe. But the earth was completely under water. Later God sent a rainbow. The rainbow was God's promise never to send such a flood again.

Remember:
God wants you to love Him.

from the Old Testament

A Very Tall Building

Noah's family grew bigger and bigger. All the people in the world were now living near the town of Babel. They started thinking. What if they could build a building so tall it would touch the sky? Then they could rule over the rest of the world, just like God!

Blocks made from dirt were placed on top of each other. The building grew taller and taller. But God was not happy.

God wanted the people to live all over His world, not in one place. So God made the people start speaking differently. They couldn't understand each other, and they couldn't finish the building. Soon they moved away from Babel.

Remember:
God knows what is best
for you.

from the Old Testament

Can You Number the Stars?

Not too far from Babel was the home of a man named Abraham. Like Noah, Abraham loved God, and God loved Abraham.

God told Abraham to pack everything he owned and begin a long trip. Finally, Abraham's family settled in what is now the country of Israel. God told them this would be their home forever. God also said Abraham would be the father of a people that would number more than all the stars in the sky!

How could this happen? Abraham and his wife Sarah had no children and besides, they were around 100 years old. But God always tells the truth and soon Abraham and Sarah had a little boy named Isaac.

Remember:
God always keeps His
promises.

from the Old Testament

No One Has a Coat Like Joseph's!

Abraham's family grew and grew. Isaac had twin sons, and one of them, Jacob, had twelve sons! Jacob loved all his sons, but Joseph was his favorite. He loved him so much he gave him a coat with all the colors you can name.

Joseph's brothers were mad. They wanted to be Jacob's favorite sons, too. So they did something very bad. They sold Joseph to some men from another land, and those men took Joseph away.

But God loved Joseph. God had a plan for him. One day Joseph would be a powerful ruler in Egypt. One day Joseph and his brothers and father would be together again.

Remember:
God is always with you.

from the Old Testament

Moses Is the Leader

Four hundred years passed and Joseph and his brothers' great-great-great-grandchildren still lived in Egypt. They were called the **Hebrews** and they were now slaves. Every day they had to work very, very hard but they still loved God.

God chose one man to lead the Hebrews back to the land of Abraham. His name was Moses.

God told Moses to talk to the king of Egypt. But the king would not let the people leave. Terrible things happened. Frogs, flies, and bugs were everywhere!

Finally the king said yes. God made a sea turn into land so the Hebrews could escape. But Moses and the Hebrews had a long way to go.

Remember:
God has something special
for you to do, too.

from the Old Testament

A City Falls Down

As the Hebrews, now called **Israelites,** entered the land of Abraham they had a big problem. The city of Jericho with its very high walls would have to be conquered. But how?

God told Joshua, the Israelites' new leader, just how to do it. First, Joshua and the people marched in a big circle once around Jericho. Some blew on horns but no one spoke. Every day for the next six days the Israelites did this.

On the seventh day they marched seven times around the city walls and stopped. Then Joshua yelled, "Shout! The Lord has given you the city!" Suddenly, the walls of Jericho crashed down!

Remember:
God can do anything
and everything.

from the Old Testament

The Strongest Man

Sometimes the Israelites forgot about God. Sometimes their land was taken by other peoples like the evil Philistines. You wouldn't want to meet a Philistine.

But God had not forgotten the Israelites. God chose a man named Samson to save Israel.

God had made Samson very strong. Samson was so strong he could kill a lion with his hands! But Samson had a secret: If he got a haircut his strength would be gone. One day that happened and the Philistines captured Samson. But Samson's hair grew back. At a big party Samson pulled a building down on top of thousands of Philistines.

Remember:
God will never forget you.

from the Old Testament

Ruth Meets Boaz

Ruth and her mother-in-law Naomi were living in the town of Bethlehem. They had no husbands (they had died), no food, and no money! But things were not so bad. Ruth and Naomi loved God. They were not alone.

One of Naomi's relatives was a man named Boaz. Boaz owned what you would call a farm. When Ruth came to work in Boaz's fields something amazing happened. Boaz began to love Ruth, and Ruth began to love Boaz.

Soon they were married and later they had a son named Obed. Naomi was so proud of Obed!

Remember:
Love is a gift from God.

from the Old Testament

Hannah Has a B

Hannah and her husband wanted ⌐
So Hannah went to the temple to pray.
"Please, God," she said, "if You give me a son
I will give him back to You." What did that
mean? Could God hear Hannah?

God gave Hannah a son named Samuel,
and Hannah kept her promise to God. When
Samuel was around five Hannah brought him
to the temple to live with a man of God
named Eli. Eli would take good care of
Samuel.

But every year Hannah visited Samuel.
She brought him a new coat, just like the ones
Eli wore. One day Samuel would be God's
prophet. Samuel would talk to God.

Remember:
God hears every word
you say to Him,
even if you whisper.

1 Samuel 1:1-3:21

from the Old Testament

Who Will Fight a Giant?

David liked to watch his sheep and play music on his harp. To keep his sheep safe David would take his slingshot and shoot stones at wild animals.

At the time there was a war in Israel. David went to see his older brothers who were fighting. The enemy had a giant named Goliath on their side. No one in Israel's army was brave enough to fight him. No one except David. With just one stone and his slingshot David killed Goliath.

Do you remember Ruth and Boaz? They were David's great-grandparents. One day David would be king of Israel.

Remember:
You don't have to be afraid
if you love God.

from the Old Testament

Best Friends

The king of Israel was named Saul. King Saul was jealous of David. He wanted the people to like him as much as they liked David.

David knew how Saul felt so he decided to hide in a forest. While he was hiding David met Saul's son Jonathan. They promised to be best friends forever.

Later King Saul and Jonathan were killed in a war and David was finally crowned king. God loved David and while he was king Israel became very powerful. But David had not forgotten Jonathan. From then on Jonathan's son would eat at the king's table in the royal palace.

Remember:
God has promised to be
your best friend.

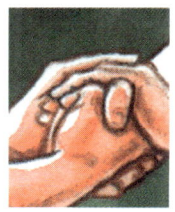

36   *from the Old Testament*

The Golden Temple

When David died his son Solomon became king. One night after Solomon said his prayers he had a dream. In his dream God told him to ask for anything he wanted and his wish would be granted. Solomon gave a good answer. He asked for wisdom, that is, being able to understand great things. Solomon wanted to be a good king.

God made Solomon the smartest king who ever lived! God also let Solomon build a temple. But this was not like any other house of God. Solomon's temple was filled with gold and brass, wood cut from cedar trees, and huge stones. Seven years were spent building the temple.

Remember:
You can ask God for
wisdom, too.

from the Old Testament

Elijah's God Is Your God

Again the Israelites forgot about God. So God sent Elijah to give a message to King Ahab.

Elijah told Ahab that there would be no rain in Israel for three years. Sure enough, not a drop of rain fell. Soon the people and animals were dying. It was time for Elijah to show the Israelites the power of God.

Elijah told Ahab to bring all his prophets to the top of a mountain. There they would have a contest. They would gather wood for two big fires, but only the one true God would light the fire. Ahab's prophets cried and sang and danced to their gods. No fire came. Then Elijah prayed, and guess what happened? Fire fell from the sky, and, in a little while, the rains came.

Remember:
There is only one God.

1 Kings 17:1-18:45

from the Old Testament

Horses of Fire

With God's power Elijah brought a little boy who had died back to life. He also caused a river to dry up by throwing his robe on the water.

When Elijah's work on earth was almost finished, God told him to find a new prophet to follow him. Elijah found a man named Elisha. Elijah gave him his robe. Suddenly, a sled or **chariot** made of fire, pulled by horses also made of fire, could be seen in the sky! The chariot swooped down and picked up Elijah and carried him up to heaven.

Elisha then took Elijah's robe and threw it on the river. Once again the river dried up. Now the power of God was with Elisha.

Remember:
God wants you to have
friends who love Him, too.

from the Old Testament

Jonah Learns
the Hard Way

Do you remember the Philistines? Well, a long time later Israel had another enemy, the people of Nineveh.

God told Jonah to go to Nineveh but that was the last place Jonah wanted to go! Instead Jonah got on a ship and sailed far away. One night at sea a tremendous storm arose. The sailors were very scared. But Jonah knew the storm had come because he had disobeyed God. Jonah was right. As soon as the sailors threw him overboard, the storm stopped.

Suddenly, Jonah was swallowed whole by a great fish! Three days later the fish spit Jonah out on a beach. Later Jonah went to Nineveh and the people there began to love God.

Remember:
You can never hide
from God.

44   *from the Old Testament*

How Old Is King Josiah?

After Ahab many kings ruled over Israel. Some were young and some were old but hardly any were as young as Josiah. He was crowned king when he was only eight years old!

When Josiah was a little older he decided to love only God and no other gods. Pretty soon everyone else in Israel loved only God, too. Josiah then ordered the temple to be made God's special house again.

Deep inside the temple some writings known as the Ten Commandments were uncovered. God had told Moses long ago to write these very words. King Josiah made all the Israelites listen to these ten best ways to live.

Remember:
God wants you to read His
Word, the Bible.

46   *from the Old Testament*

The Lions Are Hungry!

Once the Israelites had to leave their country and live in a strange land. Daniel, an Israelite who was really God's prophet, was chosen by the king of Babylon for a special job. Sometimes he could tell the king what to do.

But some men who did not like Daniel told the king to make a new law. This law said that no one could pray to their gods. These men knew that Daniel prayed to God every day.

Daniel was thrown into a den of growling, hungry lions! But an angel of God saved Daniel and the lions did not eat him. When the king found Daniel alive the next morning, he ordered everyone to worship God.

Remember:
God loves to hear your
prayers.

from the Old Testament

Esther Gives a Party

Do you like stories about kings and queens? Well, once upon a time there was a beautiful queen named Esther and she lived with her king in a big palace.

No one in the palace knew that Esther had a cousin named Mordecai. That was a good thing because one of the king's friends hated Mordecai. In fact, he wanted to kill all of Mordecai's people, the Jews!

As queen, Esther might be able to help Mordecai and save her people. She invited the king and his friend to not one but two parties where there was lots of good food. Later the king told Esther she could have anything she wanted. Esther asked that her people be saved.

Remember:
You should never hate
anyone.

from the Old Testament

Nehemiah Builds a Wall

Some Israelites had returned to Israel but they were in trouble. Israel's biggest city, Jerusalem, was being attacked because the city walls had fallen down.

Living in another land, a man named Nehemiah heard about the walls of his city. He decided to come home right away! Nehemiah got all the families in Jerusalem to help him rebuild the wall. Everybody worked so fast that the wall was built in fifty-two days.

Nehemiah then had the people listen to God's laws. They promised that day to love God forever. In 400 years God would send His Son to Israel. Until then no prophet would talk to God.

Remember:
God wants you
to help others.

New
Testament
Stories

from the New Testament

An Angel Came One Day

God's home is in heaven but God is so powerful He can be everywhere at the same time. Sometimes, though, God sends His angels to earth on special missions.

God's angel came to a man named Zacharias while he was in the temple. The angel told him that he and his wife Elizabeth would have a son named John. John would help many people to know God's Son.

A while later God's angel came to Elizabeth's cousin, a woman named Mary. The angel told Mary she would have a son, but her son would be God's Son, Jesus! God had chosen Mary over all the women in the world.

Remember:
God made you like
no one else.

from the New Testament

He Was Born in a Barn

Mary and her husband Joseph had to travel to Bethlehem, the home of their relatives Ruth and David. Do you remember them?

Since there was no room at any of the inns Mary and Joseph had to stay in a barn or **manger.** There were probably animals in this barn, cows and donkeys and maybe mice! While in the barn Mary gave birth to God's Son, Jesus.

Nearby some shepherds were taking care of their sheep. Suddenly God's angel stood before them and soon the sky was filled with singing angels. "God's Son has just been born," said the angel. "Go and meet Him!"

Remember:
You celebrate Jesus' birthday
at Christmas.

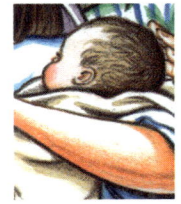

from the New Testament

They Follow a Star

Before Jesus was born a new star had appeared in the night sky. Some men from a faraway land, known as **wise men,** decided to follow this star. A new star meant a king was about to be born!

Traveling on camels, the wise men followed the star to the baby Jesus. They unpacked their gifts of gold and spices and bowed down before God's Son. These were gifts for a king, and Jesus is King of heaven and earth.

Soon Mary and Joseph became afraid someone might hurt Jesus. They decided to leave the country. Later they would live in the city of Nazareth.

Remember:
Jesus was once a baby
like you.

from the New Testament

When Jesus Was Twelve

When Jesus was growing up only Mary and Joseph knew that He was God's Son. Soon others would see that Jesus was not like other boys.

When he was twelve Jesus traveled to Jerusalem with many members of his family. The temple in Jerusalem was filled with Bible teachers. Jesus started spending a lot of time there. The teachers were very surprised. How could a boy of twelve ask such amazing questions? How could he give such incredible answers?

When it was time to leave Mary and Joseph couldn't find Jesus. Finally they found Him, sitting in the temple. "I was in My Father's house," Jesus said.

Remember:
Your church is God's
house, too.

Luke 2:41-50

from the New Testament

Come to the River

Zacharias and Elizabeth's son John was called John the Baptist. People came from all over to hear him talk about God and to be "baptized."

Anyone who said they loved God John would take into a river. He would then hold them under water for a short time, or **baptize** them. In a way, to baptize means to "wash away" your bad ways. You will still make mistakes but you will try to do what God wants.

One day Jesus came to this river. Jesus had not done anything bad. It was God's plan that John baptize Jesus. As Jesus came up from the water a white bird landed on Him. Then a voice from heaven—God's voice—said, "This is My Son."

Remember:
When you are baptized you
are telling everyone you
love Jesus.

from the New Testament

Only Jesus Can Do That!

Jesus performed amazing acts known as **miracles** so that people would listen to Him. He had much to teach them but He had to get their attention first.

Once Jesus made a sick boy well again even though Jesus was many miles away. One woman knew that if she only touched Jesus' robe she would be well. She was right! A man who couldn't walk had his friends break through a roof just so he could be made better by Jesus. Jesus even brought a man who had died back to life.

Jesus, the Son of God, fed thousands with a few fish, calmed a storm at sea, and even walked on water!

Remember: Everything Jesus did was good.

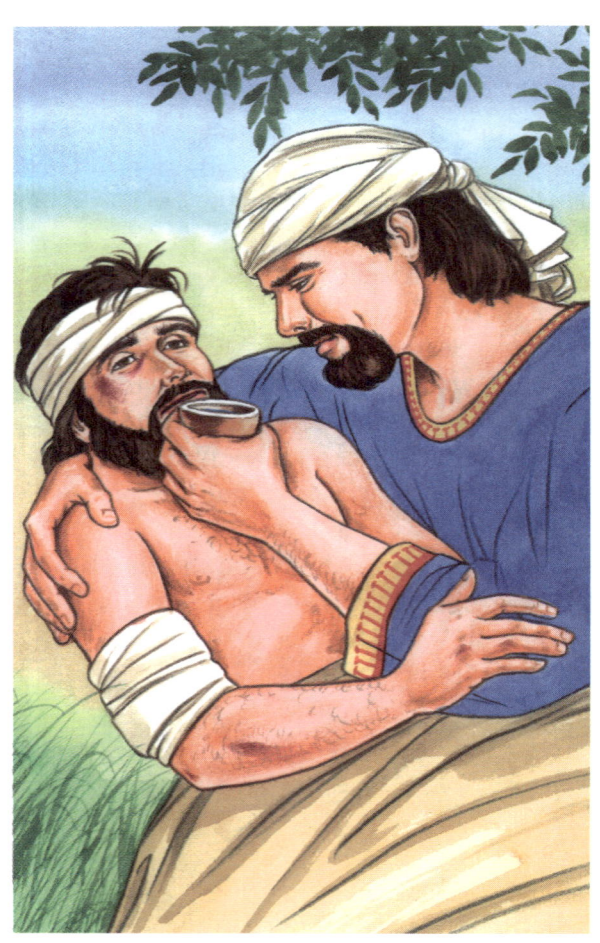

from the New Testament

Love Each Other

Jesus loved being with little kids, just like you. He loved holding them and telling them stories. Once Jesus said He watches over you like a good shepherd. Jesus knows you by name and He will always be with you.

Here's one story Jesus told. A man was traveling in the country when he was robbed and beaten by some bad men. They left him bleeding by the side of the road. Two travelers saw the man and passed by. But a third man, a Samaritan, stopped and bandaged the man. He even brought him to an inn where he paid for his care.

Jesus said we should all be like the Samaritan. We should love each other.

Remember:
Always be kind.

from the New Testament

Up a Tree

Zacchaeus had no friends. His job was to take money from the people to pay the rulers. Sometimes, though, Zacchaeus took too much money and kept some for himself.

One day Jesus visited Zacchaeus's city. Crowds of people were there to see Him. Because Zacchaeus was short the only way he could see Jesus was to climb up a tree. When Jesus passed by underneath all of a sudden He looked up and told Zacchaeus to come down. Jesus wanted to stay at the home of Zacchaeus.

That day Zacchaeus gave back all the money he had stolen, and more. That day Jesus had changed his life.

Remember:
Jesus wants you always
to tell the truth.

70   *from the New Testament*

Hosanna!

There were no cars or trucks or buses when Jesus was on earth. People often rode donkeys to get from place to place.

Jesus told some friends where they could find a donkey for Him. Then He began to ride into Jerusalem. As He entered the city, many people gathered, throwing down their coats for Jesus to ride over. Others cut branches from palm trees and waved them as Jesus rode by. "Hosanna in the highest!" the people shouted. *Hosanna* means "save us, we pray."

These people wanted Jesus to be a king like other kings on earth. But that was not what Jesus wanted.

Remember:
Jesus wants to be King in
your heart.

from the New Testament

Jesus Says Goodbye, for Now

Soon Jesus would have to die and go back to heaven. Jesus had to die so that you can go to heaven, too. If you know deep inside that Jesus is God's Son, someday you will live forever with Him.

At a dinner called the Last Supper Jesus told His friends He had to go away. Even so, He would see them soon. Then Jesus said that someone sitting at the dinner table would turn Him over to men who would kill Him. Certain men in power didn't like Jesus saying He was God's Son.

After dinner Jesus went to a garden to pray. Soon Jesus was taken prisoner.

Remember:
If you love Jesus, someday
you will see Him.

from the New Testament

Nighttime at Noon

Jesus had done nothing wrong. He had only spoken the truth: He is the Son of God. But for that Jesus was beaten and forced to die by hanging on a wooden cross. Jesus could have walked away–He can do anything!–but He knew this was God's plan for the world.

At noon on the day Jesus died the sky turned as black as night, and stayed dark for three hours. Only God could have caused that to happen.

Jesus was buried in a large cave. Guards were placed outside to make sure no one took His body. A rock larger than any man was also placed in front of the cave.

Remember:
Jesus died for everyone.

from the New Testament

Jesus Lives Forever

Three days after Jesus died on the cross the cave where His body had lain was empty. The guards were gone; the rock had been rolled away. Where was Jesus?

Jesus had told His friends that He would be "raised from the dead." Now they knew what He was talking about! Only the Son of God could come back to life.

Jesus would spend forty more days on earth teaching His closest friends. They would have to share Jesus' words with the rest of the world.

"I am with you always," Jesus said while standing on top of a mountain. Then He rose higher and higher up into heaven.

Remember:
Jesus' home is in heaven and
in your heart, if you believe
in Him.

from the New Testament

Let's Follow the Wind

Do you know what sound the wind makes? *Whooo-whooo-whoosh!* That's the sound heard all over Jerusalem just ten days after Jesus went back to heaven.

Jesus' friends were together in an upstairs room when all of a sudden the wind could be heard. Then, flames of fire appeared above everyone in the room! The power of God was in that room.

People from many lands who were in Jerusalem started following the sound of the wind. When they met Jesus' friends they couldn't believe what they heard! They heard their own language being spoken. They heard all about Jesus. That day thousands of people began to love Jesus.

Remember:
All around the world you
can meet people who
love Jesus.

from the New Testament

Saul Can't See

Saul was an enemy of Jesus. He didn't like Jesus' friends–now called **Christians**–telling people about Jesus' life and how He died for them. Saul didn't know that Jesus loved him, too.

As Saul was traveling one day a bright light from heaven shone only on him. Saul couldn't see a thing! Then Jesus' voice could be heard: "Saul, why are you fighting Me? I am Jesus." Three days later Saul was able to see again. Three days later Saul had become a Christian himself.

Saul would later be called Paul. Paul would travel to many countries, telling as many people as he could that Jesus loves them.

Remember:
Thank God every day for
your ministers and Sunday
school teachers.

82   *from the New Testament*

Peter and Dorcas

Dorcas loved to help poor people. She would make beautiful clothes for them to wear and do nice things for them. But then Dorcas got sick and later she died.

Peter, one of Jesus' closest friends, was in a nearby town when he heard about Dorcas. He came right away to the house where her body lay. Peter then asked everyone to leave. He wanted to be alone. He wanted to pray to God.

Turning to Dorcas, Peter said, "Get up!" Dorcas opened her eyes and stood.

Since the day of the great wind God had given Peter greater power to perform miracles.

Remember:
Miracles like Peter's
are done only
by the power of God.

84   *from the New Testament*

Peter and the Angel

The Christians were in danger! They were being put in prison just because they wouldn't stop telling people about Jesus.

Now Peter was in prison and there was no way he could escape. Four guards watched him and heavy chains were around his body. Peter's friends could not see him but day and night they prayed for him.

In the middle of the night God sent an angel to Peter's prison. All of a sudden Peter's chains fell off and the angel said, "Follow me." Peter and the angel walked past the guards and out of the prison. God had set Peter free!

Remember:
God wants you to tell
others about Jesus.

from the New Testament

The Color of a King

Lydia was different from many women in the Bible. She had her own business. Lydia sold cloth fit for a king, beautiful, bright purple cloth! Is purple one of your favorite colors, too?

Little did Lydia know that soon she would know a real King. The King of our hearts, Jesus.

Do you remember Paul? Paul had a dream from God to visit Lydia's country. As he was traveling in her town Paul met Lydia and told her about Jesus. Lydia was so happy she invited Paul and his friend to stay in her house. Later Paul baptized Lydia and a church in her town was started.

Remember:
When you love Jesus
you feel happy.

from the New Testament

The Adventures of Paul

Paul was the first action hero for God!

Once God sent an earthquake to free Paul from prison. Another time an angry mob of people wanted to kill him. Because he loved Jesus, Paul spent many years in prison, often sharing the good news of Jesus with his guards. And that's not all. After a hair-raising storm Paul was shipwrecked and washed ashore on a strange island! While on the island God gave Paul the power to make all the sick people better.

God had not made Paul's life easy. Many think Paul had trouble walking. But Paul was always happy to be a Christian.

Remember:
Even if bad things happen,
God is always with you.

from the New Testament

The City of Gold

Jesus' friend John was very old. As a punishment for being a Christian John was sent to a lonely island to spend the rest of his life.

On the island God came to John in a dream. In his dream John is taken to heaven where he sees Jesus. Angels fall down in front of Jesus and everywhere beautiful music is heard. Then John sees a city almost too incredible to describe.

This city will someday be our new home. It is always daytime in this city and there is no sickness or crying. If you love Jesus, someday you will live there, too.

Remember:
Every word in the Bible is
true because God wrote all
the words.

from the New Testament

Jesus Is Coming Again!

Someday, no one knows when, Jesus is coming back to earth.

Just as He went up to heaven, He will come back to earth in the clouds, too. A trumpet will sound and all Christians living on earth will fly up to meet Jesus in the sky. Those Christians who have already died will also be with Jesus. Together all Christians will live in heaven with Jesus.

What is heaven like? God has promised us a place of many mansions and beauty beyond our imagination. God has promised us a place of no sickness or tears. God has promised us a place of singing, happiness, and love.

Remember:
The best thing you can ever
do is to love Jesus.

Psalm 23

The Lord is my shepherd;
I shall not want.
He maketh me to lie down
    in green pastures:
he leadeth me beside
    the still waters.
He restoreth my soul:
he leadeth me in the paths
    of righteousness
for his name's sake.
Yea, though I walk through
    the valley of the shadow
    of death,
I will fear no evil:
for thou art with me;
thy rod and thy staff
they comfort me.
Thou preparest a table before me
in the presence of mine enemies:

thou anointest my head with oil;
my cup runneth over.
Surely goodness and mercy
shall follow me all the days
    of my life:
and I will dwell in the house
    of the Lord for ever.

The Lord's Prayer

Our Father which art in heaven,
Hallowed be thy name.
Thy kingdom come. Thy will be done
in earth, as it is in heaven.
Give us this day our daily bread
And forgive us our debts,
as we forgive our debtors.
And lead us not
into temptation,
but deliver us
from evil:
For thine is the
kingdom,
and the
power,
and the
glory,
for ever.
Amen.

Matthew 6:9-13